Nat Ran

by Sofia Martinez
illustrated by Annie Pathak

Decodable 20

Mc Graw Hill Education

Bothell, WA • Chicago, IL • Columbus, OH • New York, NY

MHEonline.com

Send all inquiries to:
McGraw-Hill Education
8787 Orion Place
Columbus, OH 43240

ISBN: 978-0-02-135312-5
MHID: 0-02-135312-3

Printed in China

9 10 11 12 13 DSS 28 27 26 25 24

Mud!

Nat got in mud.

So, Nan got a big, tan tub.
Then Nat hid.

Nan got a hose.
Nan made suds.

Dan had a bag.

He had rags.

Then Nat ran fast.

Can Dan and Nan grab him?

Nat got mud on Nan and Dan!